THE MAN ON WALL STREET

*A Deep Dive
into the World of Investment*

TANNAY KUMAR

INDIA • SINGAPORE • MALAYSIA

Notion Press Media Pvt Ltd

No. 50, Chettiyar Agaram Main Road,
Vanagaram, Chennai, Tamil Nadu – 600 095

First Published by Notion Press 2021
Copyright © Tannay Kumar 2021
All Rights Reserved.

ISBN 978-1-63997-503-7

This book has been published with all efforts taken to make the material error-free after the consent of the author. However, the author and the publisher do not assume and hereby disclaim any liability to any party for any loss, damage, or disruption caused by errors or omissions, whether such errors or omissions result from negligence, accident, or any other cause.

While every effort has been made to avoid any mistake or omission, this publication is being sold on the condition and understanding that neither the author nor the publishers or printers would be liable in any manner to any person by reason of any mistake or omission in this publication or for any action taken or omitted to be taken or advice rendered or accepted on the basis of this work. For any defect in printing or binding the publishers will be liable only to replace the defective copy by another copy of this work then available.

DEDICATION

To My Parents & Friends,
for inspiring me into believing that
anything is possible.

Contents

Acknowledgement..7

Chapter 1	Investment	9
Chapter 2	The Primary & Secondary Market	 17
Chapter 3	Derivatives	 21
Chapter 4	Banks & Depositories	 25
Chapter 5	Securities	 27
Chapter 6	Mutual Funds	 29
Chapter 7	Risk Management	 37
Chapter 8	Trading	 41
Chapter 9	Futures and Options	 45
Chapter 10	Indian Government Regulatory Framework	 47

Chapter 11	Fundamental Analysis	53
Chapter 12	Technical Analysis	61
Chapter 13	Financial Statement Analysis	69
Chapter 14	Clearing and Settlement	81
Chapter 15	Measures of Central Tendency	87

Acknowledgement

Multiple pices of information, images have been extracted from The National Stock Exchange Hand Book.

Chapter 1

Investment

An investment is an act of allocating money and resources to get returns.

A person should invest:

- To gain returns on idle savings.
- Generate an amount in a specific period.
- Maximise savings for an unstable future.
- **The most important reason to invest is to fight inflation.**

Inflation – Inflation is the rise of the price, which causes the value of money to reduce. A decline in the purchasing power of the currency overtime

- It is good to invest soon as it gives your investment more time to grow.
- It is better to invest long term and not short term.

- If you invest long term, the compounding concept will increase your income.

"I bought my first share at the age of 11 years, and even then it was too late!"

– Warren Buffet

10 Important Steps A Person Should Keep In Mind While Investing:

1. Obtaining written documents explaining the investment
2. Read and understand documents related to the investment
3. Verify the legitimacy of the investment
4. Analyse the costs and benefits related to the investment
5. Evaluate the risk and return profile of the investment
6. Evaluate the liquidity and safety of the investment
7. Determine whether the investment is appropriate for your goal
8. Compare multiple investment options

9. Seek all clarification
10. Deal Through an authorised (SEBI Registered) intermediary

Interest:

- Interest is a fee a borrower pays to use the lender's money.
- The interest is some per cent of the principal amount lent.
- The interest can be for loan life or depending on the terms and conditions of the loan.

4 Main Factors That Determine Interest Rates:

- Rates banks offer to depositors.
- Rates banks offer to borrowers.
- Rates of the government securities.
- Rates offered to investors in small saving schemes.

3 Main Factors That Effect Interest Rates:

- Demand for money.
- Supply for money.
- Inflation rate.

An asset is a property that an economic entity owns and manages. It can be used to create wealth and is part of the entity's net worth and can generate positive economic value.

A liability is a debt that an individual or corporation owes to another party, generally in the form of loans, accounts payable, mortgages are also examples of liabilities.

A person can invest in 2 types of assets, physical assets and financial assets.

Financial Assets include any intangible financial securities

Examples of A Few Financial Assets Are:

- Life Insurance
- Equity Shares
- Debt Shares (Bonds/Debentures)
- Mutual Funds
- Public Provident Funds
- Saving Bank Account
- Money Market Fund
- Bank Fixed Deposits
- Etcetera.

Physical Assets include any tangible securities.

Examples of A Few Physical Assets Are:

- Land
- Building
- Machinery
- Equipment
- Gold
- Patents
- Commodities
- Post Stamps
- Etcetera.

Examples of short term and long term investment options:

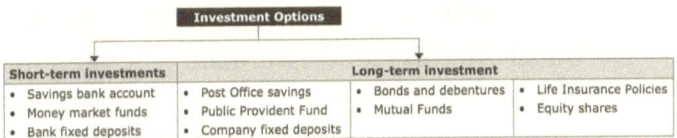

The Image Above Shows Different Types Of Investment Options Both Short-term & Long-term

Equity Share

An equity share is an ordinary share that represents fractional ownership of a company with voting rights in the company.

There are five types of equity shares:

- Right Issue Shares – The issue of new securities to existing shareholders at a ratio to those already held.

- Bonus Shares – Shares issued to stakeholder by a company free of cost based on the number of shares they already own.

- Preference Shares – Preference shares are equity shares, but preference shareholders are paid first when a dividend is announced.

- Cumulative Preference Shares – Cumulative preference shares are preference shares, but if the dividend is unpaid, the amount gets accumulated.

- Cumulative Convertible Preference Shares – Cumulative Convertible Preference Shares are Cumulative preference shares converted to equity shares after a certain point in time.

Debt Shares

Debt shares represent a contract where one entity money/resources to another entity on predetermined terms concerning rate, periodic interest and repayment of the lent amount.

Bond: In the Indian securities market, the term bond refers to a debt instrument or debt share issued by the central and state governments and public sector organisations

Debentures: In the Indian securities market, the term debentures refers to a debt instrument or debt share issued by the private corporate sector.

Features of debt shares:

- Maturity: A bond's maturity refers to when the borrower has agreed to repay all principals with interest.

- Coupon: Coupon refers to the periodic interest payment that the borrower makes to the lender.

- Principal: The principal is the borrowed amount or the face value of a debt share.

Chapter 2

The Primary & Secondary Market

The Primary Market:

- The primary Market is a channel where entities can sell new securities

- It also provides an opportunity for investors to security issuers, government as well as corporations to raise resources to meet their requirements

- They may issue securities at face value or discount/premium

- These securities can be in multiple forms, for example, equity in the company or debt

- The securities can be Issued in domestic or the international markets

- The issuance of security takes place as a public issue or a private issue

- A public entity is not limited to several investors

- A private entity is limited to 200 investors.
- If a private entity has more than 200 investors, the entity has to declare itself as public

IPO – Initial Public Offering

An initial public offering offers a private companies stock on a public stock exchange for the first time. The offering price of an IPO is the price at which a company sells its shares to investors. Thus, it helps decide the price band of a private companies share price.

The Secondary Market:

- The secondary market is where you trade securities of a public listed corporation or any company listed on the stock exchange.
- Major and most trades are made in the secondary market
- Secondary markets do not issue any equity and debt shares. Only trading takes place
- Participants that hold securities can adjust their response concerning market risk and the return value they will attain.

- They are also allowed to sell their securities to meet liquidity needs
- The secondary market also has an over the counter Market and exchange
- OTC is a market where trades are negotiated
- All on the spot trades for immediate delivery and payment take place here

Contract Note

A contact note is a confirmation of trades done on a particular day on behalf of the client by a trading member. It imposes a legal relation between the client and the trading member concerning buying, selling and settling trade.

Contents of A Contract Note:

- Name, Address and SEBI registration number trading member (broker)
- Name of the partner and Signature Dealing Office Address
- Contract Number
- Client Name
- Client Code

- Order Number/Time
- Trade Number/Time Quantity and kind of security Brokerage & Purchase
- Service Tax
- Appropriate Stamps Signature of Broker

A portfolio is a combination of different investment assets mixed and matched to log the investors investment. Items that are considered a pair of your portfolio can include any asset you own:

- shares
- debentures
- bonds
- mutual funds
- Et cetera...

Chapter 3

Derivatives

Derivates are products whose value is derived from one or more basic variables called underlying assets.

There are 3 types of derivatives:

- Forwards: A forward contract is a customised contract between two entities in which a settlement takes place on a specific date in the future at the current times the predetermined price.

- Futures: A futures contract is a certain type of forwarding contract because the former are standardised exchange traded contracts, such as futures of the Nifty index.

- Options: An option is a type of contract which provides rights to buy or sell the underlying at a specific date and a specific price. The buyer of an option has to pay a fee and buy the right to use the option the writer of the option gets the fees and has to buy and sell the assets for the option holder.

There are 4 types of options:

- European Options: European Options are options that can only be exercised on the expiry date

- American options: American Options are options that can be exercised any time up to and including the expiry date

- Bermuda option: Bermuda option are Options that can only be practised on predetermined dates it is a mix of American and European options.

- Warrants: Options generally have a life of up to one year. Warrants are options with a more extended validity period.

The FCRA Forward Contracts (Regulation) Act, 1952 defines commodities as "every kind of movable property other than actionable claims, money and securities". Therefore, trading in such goods/commodities is permitted by the Central Government.

The commodities exchange is an organisation or corporation of any other corporate organising futures trading in commodities. In the broader sense, it is taken to include any organised marketplace where trade is routed through one mechanism, allowing effective competition among buyers and sellers.

The commodities derivative market trade in contracts in which the underlying asset is a commodity. The commodity can be agricultural for example wheat, soybeans, rapeseed, cotton, etc. or other natural elements like gold, silver, etc.

Chapter 4

Banks & Depositories

A depository can be compared to a bank the function of a depository and bank is similar.

BANK	DEPOSITORY
Holds funds in an account	Hold securities in an account
Transfers funds between accounts on the instruction of the account holder	Transfers securities between accounts on the instruction of the account holder.
Facilitates transfers without having to handle money	Facilitates transfers of ownership without having to handle securities.
Facilitates safekeeping of money	Facilitates safekeeping of shares.

The above image provides information about banks and depositories

- A depository is a location where everything is stored for storing or safeguarding, such as a building, office, or warehouse.

- Depositories may be companies, banks, or other entities that store shares and help with trading.

- They deliver stability and liquidity and the ability to lend capital to others, invest in shares, and send money.

ISIN – An ISIN number is an International Securities Identification Number is a unique identification number a to a security by a depository.

2 depositories provide dematerialisation in India the NSDL (National Securities Depository Limited) and the CDSL (Central Depository Services)

Chapter 5

Securities

According to the securities contract regulation act (SCRA) 1956, A security is any kind of tradable financial asset that could generate wealth. Thus, securities include stocks, bonds, scrips, etcetera.

The securities market is where buyers and sellers of securities can enter into transactions to purchase and sell shares, bonds, debentures, etcetera. It helps and enables corporates and entrepreneurs to raise resources for their companies and ventures through public issues.

The securities market needs regulators to ensure that the market participants behave in a desired manner so that the securities market continues to be a significant source of finance.

The securities market is regulated by 4 significant bodies:

- The department of economic affairs (DEA)
- The department of company affairs (DCA)

- The reserve bank of India (RBI)
- The securities exchange board of India (SEBI)

It is essential to transact through a government registered intermediary.

The securities market is divided into 2 different segments the primary Market and the secondary Market. The primary Market provides a channel of new securities issues and the secondary market deals with previously issued securities.

Chapter 6

Mutual Funds

The regulatory body of mutual funds is SEBI. A the mutual funds get registered with the stock exchange board of India.

There are multiple benefits of investing in mutual funds like:

- Small Investment – With minimal investments, mutual funds can help you recognise the benefits of a portfolio diversified across a wide range of securities.

- Professional Fund Management – A mutual fund's pool of money is managed by professionals with significant expertise, experience, and resources. They conduct extensive research into the markets and the economy in order to identify promising investment opportunities.

- Spreading Risk – With limited finances, an investor may be able to invest in only one or two stocks/bonds, increasing risk.

A mutual fund, on the other hand, will diversify its risk by investing in a variety of safe equities and bonds. A fund typically invests in companies from a variety of industries to diversify risk.

- Transparency – Mutual funds give investors with updates on the value of their investments on a regular basis. Mutual funds also provide a thorough portfolio disclosure of the investments made by various schemes, as well as the proportion of each asset type invested in.

- Choice – The enormous number of Mutual Funds available provide investors with a wide range of options. A scheme can be chosen by an investor according on his risk/return profile.

- Regulation – All mutual funds are registered with SEBI and operate under a set of tight regulations designed to safeguard the investor's interests.

Mutual funds do not provide assured returns. Their returns are linked to their performance they invest in shares, debentures, bonds etc. All these investments involve an element of risk.

Some of the risks mutual funds are exposed to are:

Market risk – If the value of stock or bond assets in the fund's portfolio falls due to prevailing economic circumstances, the fund's performance will be impacted.

Non-market risk – Bad news about a particular firm can cause its stock price to drop, which can have a negative impact on fund holdings. This risk can be mitigated by investing in a diversified portfolio that includes a wide range of equities from various industries.

Interest rate risk – Interest rates and bond prices move in opposite directions. Bond prices fall when interest rates rise, and this drop in underlying assets has a negative impact on the fund.

Credit Risk – Bonds are a type of debt obligation. When funds invest in corporate bonds, they bear the risk of the company defaulting on its interest and principal payment commitments, and when that risk materialises, the bond's value plummets, leading the fund's NAV to plummet.

There are multiple type of mutual funds which are classified into 2 Objective based and Flexibility based.

A few Objective based Mutual Funds are:

- Equity Funds/Growth Funds – Equity funds are mutual funds that invest in stock. They are primarily concerned with the investment's capital appreciation throughout the medium to long term. They are great for investors looking for a return on their money. Diversified funds, Sector specific funds, and Index based funds are all examples of equity funds.

- Diversified funds – These funds invest in a variety of companies from various industries. These funds are designed for risk-averse investors who want a well-balanced portfolio across industries.

- Sector funds – These funds primarily invest in equity shares of companies in a specific industry or business sector. These funds are aimed towards investors who are bullish on a certain sector's future.

- Index funds – These funds follow the same investment strategy as significant market indices as the CNX Nifty or the CNX 500. The money raised from investors is only invested in the stocks that make up the index. A Nifty index fund, for example, will only invest in the Nifty 50 stocks. The goal of such funds is not to outperform the Market, but to provide a return that is comparable to market returns.

- Tax Saving Funds – The Income Tax Act provides tax advantages to investors in these funds. This scheme provides opportunities in the form of tax rebates under the Income Tax Act.

- Debt/Income Funds – These funds primarily invest in high-rated fixed-income instruments such as bonds, debentures, government securities, commercial paper, and other money market products with a high credit rating. They are best suited for medium – to long-term investors who are risk cautious and want to protect their wealth. They provide the investor with a steady stream of revenue.

- Liquid Funds/Money Market Funds – These funds invest in money market securities that are highly liquid. The investment period could be as short as one day. They make it simple to get money. They have risen to prominence as a higher-yielding option to savings and short-term fixed deposit accounts. These funds are suited for corporations, institutional investors, and businesses looking to invest for a limited period of time.

- Gilt Funds – These funds invest in securities issued by the federal and state governments. Because they are supported by the Government, they provide a safe return while also ensuring the protection of the principal. They are suitable for risk-averse investors with a medium to long time horizon.

- Balanced Funds – In some proportions, these funds invest in both equities and fixed-income-bearing assets (debt). They give a consistent return and lessen the fund's volatility while also giving some capital appreciation potential. They are best for investors with a medium to long time horizon and a willingness to face moderate risks.

A few Flexibility based Mutual Funds are:

- Open-ended Funds – There is no set date for redemption for these monies. Subscriptions and redemptions are generally available throughout the year.

Their pricing are based on the net asset value of the day (NAV). They are far more liquid in the eyes of investors than closed-ended funds.

- Close-ended Funds – These funds are open for entry during the Initial Public Offering (IPO) and then closed for entry and exit thereafter. These funds have a set redemption date. One of the hallmarks of closed-ended schemes is that they are typically traded at a discount to NAV; however, as maturity approaches, the gap narrows. These monies are only available for subscription once and can only be redeemed on the specified redemption date. These funds' units are listed on stock exchanges (with a few exceptions), are tradable, and subscribers can exit the fund at any moment via the secondary Market.

There are 2 investment plans that mutual funds offer:

- Growth Plan and Dividend Plan
- Dividend Reinvestment Plan

Chapter 7

Risk Management

Risk management is the process of identifying, analysing, and accepting or mitigating uncertainty in investment decisions in the financial world. Risk management is defined as the process by which an investor or fund manager evaluates and attempts to quantify the potential for losses in an investment, such as a moral hazard, and then takes the necessary action (or inaction) based on the fund's investment objectives and risk tolerance.

Return is inextricably linked to risk. Every investment carries some level of risk, which can range from near zero in the case of a US T-bill to extremely high in the case of emerging-market equities or real estate in high-inflationary environments. Risk can be measured in both absolute and relative levels. A thorough grasp of risk in its various manifestations can aid investors in better comprehending the opportunities, trade-offs, and costs associated with various investing strategies.

We tend to associate the word "risk" with negative connotations. Risk, on the other hand, is required and inextricably linked to good success in the financial sector.

A variation from an expected outcome is a standard definition of investment risk. This variation might be expressed in absolute terms or relative to something else, such as a market benchmark.

While the variance could be excellent or negative, most investment professionals agree that it reflects some degree of the desired outcome for your assets. As a result, in order to earn more significant profits, one must be willing to take on more risk. It is also a widely held belief that higher risk is accompanied by increased volatility. While investing professionals are always looking for — and occasionally finding — strategies to reduce volatility, there is no clear consensus among them on how to achieve it.

The amount of volatility an investor should take is totally dependent on the investor's risk tolerance, or, in the case of an investment professional, the amount of tolerance their investment objectives allow. Standard deviation, a statistical measure of dispersion around a central tendency, is one of the most often used absolute risk indicators. You look at an investment's average return and then calculate its average standard deviation over the same time period. The predicted return of the investment is likely to be one standard deviation from the average 67 per cent of the time and two standard deviations from the average deviation 95 per cent of the time, according to normal distributions (the familiar bell-shaped curve). This aids investors in calculating risk. They invest if they believe they can withstand the financial and emotional danger.

For example, the S& P 500's average annualised total return for a 15-year period, from August 1, 1992, to July 31, 2007, was 10.7%. This figure tells what occurred throughout the course of the entire period, but it does not reveal what occurred along the way. For the same time period, the S& P 500's average standard deviation was 13.5 per cent. This is the difference between the average return and the actual return over the 15-year period at the most provided points.

Any given outcome should fall within one standard deviation of the mean around 67 per cent of the time and within two standard deviations about 95 per cent of the time when using the bell curve model. Thus, an investor in the S&

P 500 could expect a return of 10.7% plus or minus the standard deviation of 13.5 per cent roughly 67 per cent of the time; he could also assume a 27 per cent (two standard deviations) gain or reduction of 95 per cent of the time. He invests if he can afford to lose.

The Above example was obtained from Investopedia.

Chapter 8

Trading

The exchange of products and services between two entities is referred to as trading. It is the fundamental idea that underpins all economic systems and financial transactions.

Any society's wheels of growth are governed by trade, which allows for the accumulation of riches. A market is a location where any type of transaction can take place. The Market is determined based on the type of goods. The stock market, for example, is a location where stock trading takes place.

The Market is divided into two types: organised and unorganised. A regulated market is one that has a set of rules and regulations that every entity functioning in the Market must follow, and it usually has a regulatory agency to ensure that they are followed. An unorganised market lacks strict rules and regulations, and even if it had, compliance was not required.

The process of trading and investing has become considerably more convenient thanks to Internet trading and investing, with most markets being mimicked on the internet.

Trade has existed for as long as humanity has existed. Trading, on the other hand, has taken on different forms in different communities. Because of isolated human settlements that prevented union into a single system.

However, in the past, a form of commerce that was common across communities was the barter system, in which services and products were exchanged for other services and goods.

However, due to the lack of a basic standard of measurement for product worth, the barter system was discovered to be inconvenient. This inconvenient situation paved the way for money, which served as a benchmark against which all products' worth are compared.

This discovery sparked a series of economic and financial advances, including the introduction of credit, stock trading, and so on.

Stock trading began with the development of European joint-stock corporations and played an essential role in European imperialism. In recent years, informal stock exchanges have sprung up in a number of European locations. The Dutch East India Firm was the first joint-stock company to issue shares for public trading through the Amsterdam Stock Exchange.

Types of Trading:

- Day Trading – This type of trading entails buying and selling equities in the same day.

- Scalping – Micro-trading is another name for it. Intraday trading includes both scalping and day trading.

- Swing Trading – This stock market trading strategy is utilised to profit on short-term stock movements and patterns.

- Momentum Trading – In momentum trading, a trader takes advantage of a stock's momentum.

Chapter 9

Futures and Options

Futures and options are the two most common stock derivatives traded on a stock exchange. These are agreements between two parties to trade a stock asset at a later date for a preset price. By locking in a price ahead of time, these contracts attempt to mitigate market risks associated with stock market trading.

In the stock market, futures and options are contracts that draw their price from an underlying asset (also known as underlying), such as shares, stock market indices, commodities, ETFs, and other assets. Individuals can use futures and options basics to limit future risk with their investments by investing at predetermined prices. However, because the direction of price movements cannot be foreseen, a market prediction that is incorrect might result in significant profits or losses. Individuals who are familiar with the workings of a stock market are more likely to engage in such transactions.

Difference between Futures and Options:

In terms of the obligations put on individuals, future and option trading are distinct. While futures impose a burden on an investment by requiring him or her to complete a contract by a predetermined deadline, an options contract allows an individual the option to do so.

A futures contract to purchase or sell an underlying security must be followed up on at a contractual price on a predetermined date. An options contract, on the other hand, gives a buyer the chance to do the same if he or she makes a profit on a deal.

Types of Futures and Options:

While both buyers and sellers of a futures contract must follow the same rules, an options derivative can be separated into two groups. A put option contract is used by people who want to sell a specific asset at a predetermined price at a later date. Individuals who want to buy a particular asset in the future can also use a call option to lock in a price for future exchange.

Hedgers, Speculators and Arbitrageurs should mainly invest in futures and options.

Chapter 10

Indian Government Regulatory Framework

Legislations

The following are the five primary laws that govern the securities market:

1. The Securities Contracts (Regulation) Act of 1956 prohibits unfavourable securities transactions by regulating the securities business.

2. The Corporations Act of 1956, which is a unified legislation that applies to all companies in India;

3. The SEBI Act of 1992 was enacted to safeguard investors' interests as well as to promote the growth and regulation of the securities industry.

4. The Depositories Act of 1996, which governs the electronic management and transfer of ownership of dematerialised securities, was enacted in 1996.

5. Money laundering is prohibited by the Prevention of Money Laundering Act of 2002, which also provides for the seizure of property obtained from or implicated in money laundering.

Rules and Regulations

The SC(R)A, the SEBI Act, and the Depositories Act have all been amended by the Government. Under the SEBI Act and the Depositories Act, SEBI has drafted laws for the registration and regulation of all market intermediaries, as well as the prohibition of unfair trade practises and insider trading. Government and SEBI publish announcements, recommendations, and circulars under these Acts, which market players must follow. Stock exchanges and other self-regulatory organisations (SROs) have also established rules and regulations for market players.

Regulators

Regulators ensure that market participants behave in a desired manner, ensuring that the securities market remains a significant source of finance for businesses and governments while also safeguarding investors' interests. Department of Economic Affairs (DEA), Department of

Company Affairs (DCA), Reserve Bank of India (RBI), Securities and Exchange Board of India (SEBI), and Securities Appellate Tribunal (SAT) are all responsible for regulating the securities market.

Securities Contracts (Regulation) Act, 1956

The Securities Contracts (Regulation) Act of 1956 [SC(R)A] establishes direct and indirect regulation over nearly all elements of securities trading and stock exchange operations, with the goal of preventing unfavourable securities transactions. It grants the Central Government regulatory authority over (a) stock exchanges through a process of recognition and ongoing supervision, (b) securities contracts, and (c) stock exchange listings. In this part, we will go through all three of them. The Securities and Exchange Commission (R) Act of 1956 was created to avoid unfavourable securities transactions by regulating the business of dealing in securities and providing for various other things related to it. This is the primary Act that controls securities trading in India. A stock exchange must comply with the requirements set forth by the federal Government in order to be recognised.

A recognised stock exchange is where organised securities trading takes place.

Recognition of Stock Exchanges

The business of dealing in securities cannot be conducted without first registering with SEBI, according to the Act's requirements. Any Stock Exchange that wishes to be recognised must submit an application to SEBI under Section 3 of the Act, which has the authority to provide recognition and impose conditions. In the interest of the trade or the general public, this recognition might be revoked. In 2004, Section 4A of the Act was added to allow for stock exchange corporatisation and demutualisation. SEBI may establish an appointed date on and from which all recognised stock exchanges must corporatize and demutualise their stock exchanges by publication in the official gazette under section 4A of the Act. Each Recognised Stock Exchange that has not yet been corporatised and demutualised by the deadline must submit a scheme for corporatisation and demutualisation to SEBI for approval. SEBI may undertake such inquiries and acquire such information as it deems necessary after receiving the plan, and after determining that the scheme is in the best interests of the trade and the public, SEBI may approve the scheme.

Contracts and Options in Securities

A recognised stock exchange is where organised securities trading takes place. If the Central Government determines that it is necessary to do so, based on the nature or volume of securities transactions in any State or States or area, it may declare the provisions of section 13 to apply to such State or States or area by notification in the Official Gazette, and any contract entered into in such State or States or area after that date will be governed by those provisions.

Listing of Securities

When securities are listed on a person's application on a recognised stock exchange, that person must adhere to the terms of the stock exchange's listing agreement (Section 21). When a recognised stock exchange declines to list a company's shares in accordance with its bye-laws, the business has the right to be informed of the grounds for the denial, and the company has the right to appeal to the Securities Appellate Tribunal (SAT).

Delisting of Securities

Any listed company's securities may be delisted by a recognised stock exchange for any of the reasons specified in the Act. Before delisting a business from its exchange, the recognised stock exchange must provide the company with a reasonable chance to be heard and document the grounds for delisting it. The business in question, or any disgruntled investor, may file a delisting appeal with the Securities and Exchange Commission (SAT). (Section 21A of the Code of Federal Regulations)

Chapter 11

Fundamental Analysis

Fundament Analysis

Fundamental analysis examines a company's future profits potential by looking at various elements that influence the company's success. Fundamental analysis' main goal is to value a stock and purchase and sell it based on that value in the market. Economic, industry and corporate analysis are all part of the fundamental analysis. This type of analysis is frequently referred to as a top-down approach.

The value of a stock is equal to the present value of all future cash flows in the form of dividends plus the present value of the projected sale price when the equity share is sold, according to the Dividend Discount Model (DDM). The DDM implies that the dividend is paid at the same rate every year and that the first payment is received one year after the equity share is purchased.

If investors expect to hold an equity share for one year, then the current price of the share can be calculated as:

$$P_0 = \frac{D_1}{(1+r)} + \frac{P_1}{(1+r)}$$

Where

P_0 = Current price/market price of the share today

D_1 = Dividend expected at end of year 1

r = required rate of return/discount rate

P_1 = market price/expected price of share at end of year 1

Example: A company's share par value of Rs. 100 is projected to pay a 15 per cent annual dividend in the future. What is the current theoretical value (sale price) of the share if the investors' necessary rate of return on the share is 12%?

Given, Dividend = D_1 = Rs. 15; r = 12%; P_1 = 100 the current price (P_0) will be:

$$P_0 = \frac{D_1}{(1+r)} + \frac{P_1}{(1+r)} = \frac{15}{1.12} + \frac{100}{1.12} = \text{Rs. } 102.68$$

Constant Growth DDM:

Constant Growth DDM presumes that the dividend per share is growing at a constant rate (g).

The value of the share (P0) can be calculated as:

$$P_0 = \frac{D_1}{r-g}$$

Where,

D_1 = Dividend per share at the end of first year.

r = Expected rate of return/Discount rate

g = Constant growth rate

Example: On its par value of Rs. 100, the firm is anticipated to pay a 15 per cent p.a. dividend with a growth rate of 5% in the future. What is the theoretical value of the share if the necessary rate of return is 12 per cent?

$$P_0 = \frac{15}{(0.12 - 0.05)} = \frac{15}{0.07} = Rs.\,214.29$$

Economic Analysis

It is critical to examine the economic activity in which each company engages. Profits of a firm, investor attitudes, expectations, and the value of a share are all affected by economic activity.

Economic Indicators

- Global Economy

  o The world and domestic economies are the starting points for a company's top-down examination. Globalisation has an impact on a company's export potential, pricing competitiveness, and currency exchange rate.

- Domestic Economy

  o GDP: GDP is a measure of an economy's total output of goods and services. A growing GDP shows that the economy is increasing. Agriculture, as well as industrial and service output, have an impact on the Indian economy. A healthy and regular monsoon means good and average agricultural production and rising farmer and agricultural labour income. Data on industrial production show the state of industrial activity in the country.

  o Employment: The unemployment rate is the percentage of the country's entire workforce that is unemployed. The unemployment rate reflects how the economy performs when it is operating at total capacity.

o Inflation: Inflation is defined as the increase in the overall level of prices. A high inflation rate implies that the economy is running at total capacity, with demand for goods and services outstripping supply. Therefore, the Government should attempt to strike a balance between inflation and unemployment to boost employment while lowering inflation.

o Interest Rates: Because the present value of cash flows is determined by the interest rate, a high-interest rate affects demand for homes and high-value consumer durables. Therefore, the actual interest rate is a crucial component in company operations.

o Budget Deficit: The gap between government expenditure and receipts is known as the budget deficit. A more significant budget deficit means more borrowing by the Government, which raises interest rates. If government borrowing continues uncontrolled, it will crowd out private borrowing. The fiscal deficit is the sum of the budget deficit and borrowing. A more significant budget deficit suggests that the Government is spending more money on non-productive activities.

o Other Factors: Manufacturing and trade sales, Money supply, Fiscal Policy, Monetary Policy Productivity of labour, Consumer Expectations Index, Corporations are acquiring new factories and machinery. Prices of stocks, Personal earnings, Government tax revenues, FII and FDI investments, credit offtakes, and so on.

Industry Analysis

Economic contractions or expansions can decrease or increase stock markets, with varying relative price movements among industrial groupings. Thus, for the analyst, industry analysis necessitates knowledge of (1) the key sectors or subdivisions of overall economic activity that influence specific industries, and (2) the relative strength or weakness of a specific industry or other economic activity groupings.

Major Classifications: Basic Industries, Capital Goods, Consumer Durables, Consumer Non-Durables, Consumer Services, Energy, Financial Services, Health Care, Public Utilities, Technology, Transportation, and so on are some of the product and service categories in which the industry may be categorised.

Classification based on Business Cycles: Industry may be categorised based on how it reacts to economic ups and downs, referred to as business cycles. Growth industry, cyclical industry, defensive industry, and cyclical-growth industry are general industrial categories based on business cycles.

- Growth industry: A more excellent pace of expansion, increased profitability, and business cycle independence are all hallmarks of a growth industry. Frequently connected with technical advancements or novel methods of accomplishing tasks. For example, photography, colour television, computers, medicines, and office equipment were all growing businesses between the 1940s and 1960s. Recent growing industries include communication equipment, software, genetic engineering, and environmental/waste management.

- Cyclical industry: It is most likely to gain from a period of economic success while also suffering from a period of economic contraction. The largest cyclical industry is consumer durables.

- Defensive industry: It is most likely to gain from a period of economic success while also suffering from economic contraction. The largest cyclical industry is consumer durables.

- Other Factors: Sales and Profits in the Past Performance, government policy and regulation toward industry, labour circumstances, competitive conditions, industry life cycle, the attitude of international investors, industry share price, and so on.

Chapter 12

Technical Analysis

The value of a stock is forecasted using a risk-return framework based on the economic environment in fundamental analysis. Technical analysis is a different technique to predicting stock price behaviour. It is usually utilised as a supplement to fundamental analysis rather than as a replacement. The theory behind technical analysis is that the supply and demand for securities influences asset prices. Therefore, it finds significant patterns in previous financial data on charts and utilises those patterns to predict future prices.

Edwards and Magee formulate the basic assumptions underlying technical analysis:

- The interaction between supply and demand determines the market value of a security.

- The supply and demand of securities are governed by a variety of variables, both rational and irrational.

- The price of stocks tends to move in a trend that lasts for an extended period.
- Shifts in supply and demand create changes in trend.
- Changes in supply and demand can be seen in market activity charts sooner or later.
- Some chart patterns are prone to recurrence.

On the other hand, fundamental analysis attempts to assess a security's intrinsic worth, whereas technical analysis attempts to predict security prices rather than values.

Dow Theory

Technical analysis is based on the theories of Charles H. Dow, the first editor of the Wall Street Journal. According to Dow's concept, the stock market does not behave randomly and is impacted by three cyclical trends: primary trend, secondary or intermediate trend, and Tertiary or minor trend. Following these patterns might help you forecast the Market's overall direction. The long-term movement of prices, which can span anywhere from a few months to many years, is the primary trend. Markets are often referred to as bear or bull markets. Short-term price deviations from the underlying trend line generate secondary trends. They are only good for a few months. The secondary trend works as a brake on the primary trend, causing departures from its general bounds to be corrected. Daily swings in either direction (bull or bear) with little analytical significance are referred to as minor trends. In terms of bull and bear markets, the following tendencies are described:

- The accumulation phase is the first stage of a bull market. When prices are low and financial reports are not looking good, this is the time to buy. Farsighted investors, on the other hand, take advantage of the low prices and acquire shares.

- Increased activity, higher prices, and improved financial reporting define the second phase of the bull market. This is the time when you may make much money. However, the Market is vulnerable to a reversal at this time.

- The distribution phase is the first stage of a bear market. Farsighted investors can see ignorant investors racing to acquire shares at this point. Next, long-term investors begin to sell their holdings. Oversupply causes prices to fall, making profits more challenging to come by.

- Near-panic selling characterises the second phase of the bear market. Prices are falling faster than ever before, and more individuals are selling their stocks.

- The third phase of the bear market is marked by increased price loss and weakness. Lower-quality concerns are erasing the gains made during the last bull market. There is a lot of terrible market news in the news these days.

The second element of the Dow Theory states that for a credible market direction signal, the Industrial Average and the Railroad Average must confirm each other's direction. Dow developed the Industrial Average, which includes the top blue chip firms and a second average that includes the top railroad stocks (now the Transport Average). He felt that the averages' behaviour represented the whole Market's expectations and concerns. Markets all across the world exhibit the same patterns of behaviour that he saw. (At the time of Dow's writing, the Railroad Average was the sole option.) Dow Jones & Company expanded this to include truckers and airlines in 1969, and the Industrial Average and the Transportation Average now reflect it. Large active equities, according to Dow theory, will typically follow market averages. Individual issues, on the other hand, may differ from the general averages due to unique circumstances. The makeup of the particular averages is based on the fact that both the industrials and the transportations are independent. Industrialists, on the other hand, must rely on transportation to get their goods to Market. Therefore, when the industrial sector thrives, so will the transportation sector. A divergence, on the other hand, occurs when one sector does significantly better than the other. This shows that one sector is significantly more robust than the other, and if this trend continues without the other sector catching up, the Market will see a significant reversal.

The Dow Theory also says that just closing prices should be utilised. Because closing prices represent the price at which knowledgeable investors are ready to hold positions overnight, this is the case.

As a result, Dow theory is used to predict market reversals and trends and individual securities. The central concept of Dow theory is that trend and volume of shares traded have a positive connection.

Charts

During individual stock analysis, charting is an essential job for a technical analyst. Based on past price-volume data, a stock's likely future performance may be forecasted, and emerging and changing patterns of price behaviour can be recognised. Three types of charts are used in technical analysis. There are three types of graphs: (a) line graphs, (b) bar graphs, and (3) point and figure graphs. The line charts show the lines that link the prices of subsequent days. Vertical bars reflect each day's price change in the bar charts. Each bar represents the distance between the day's peak and lowest prices, with a tiny cross indicating the closing price. Line and bar charts are simpler than point and figure charts. Not only are point and figure charts used to spot trend reversals, but they are also used to anticipate price goals. This is because point and figure charts show the only significant price changes. Three or five point price changes are displayed; for low-priced securities, just one point price changes are posted. While line and bar charts have two dimensions, each vertical column representing a trading day, point and figure charts see each column as a significant reversal rather than a trading day.

Chapter 13

Financial Statement Analysis

The Balance Sheet, Profit and Loss Account, Sources and Uses of Funds Statements, and Auditors' Notes to the Financial Statements make up a financial statement. The balance sheet depicts the company's financial situation at a given point in time. The profit and loss account (Income Statement) depicts the firm's financial performance over time. The sources and uses of funds statements depict the company's movement over a specific period.

Balance Sheet, The balance sheet of a company, according to the Companies Act, should be either in account form or the report form.

Balance Sheet: Account Form

Liabilities	Assets
Share Capital	Fixed Assets
Reserves and Surplus	Investments
Secured loans	Current Assets, loans and Advances
Unsecured loans	Miscellaneous expenditure
Current liabilities and provisions	

Liability

- Share Capital – There are two types of capital in a company: equity capital and preference capital. The share capital represents the contribution of the company's owners. The dividend rate on equity capital is not fixed. The preference capital represents preference shareholders' contributions and has a predetermined dividend rate.

- Reserves and Surplus – The gains retained in the company are referred to as reserves and surpluses. Revenue reserves and capital reserves are two types of reserves. Revenue reserves are accumulated retained earnings from business operational profits. Capital reserves are assets that have been amassed that are unrelated to corporate operations. Capital reserves include things like premiums on new stock and gains on asset revaluation.

- Secured and Unsecured Loans – Borrowings secured by a security are referred to as secured loans. They take the form of debentures, financial institution loans, and commercial bank loans. Unsecured loans are those that do not require any type of collateral. Fixed deposits, promoter loans and advances, intercorporate borrowings, and unsecured bank loans are all examples.

- Current Liabilities and Provisions – They include debts owed to credit suppliers of goods and services, advances received, accumulated expenses, unclaimed dividends, tax provisions, dividends, gratuities, pensions, and so on.

Assets

- Fixed Assets: These assets are purchased long-term and employed for company operations, but they are not intended for resale. Fixed assets include land and buildings, plant and machinery, patents, and copyrights.

- Investments: Financial securities, either long-term or short-term, are considered investments. Accordingly, investment income and gains are not derived from business operations.

- Current Assets, Loans, and Advances: This includes cash and other resources that can be turned to cash throughout operations.

Current assets are assets that are retained for a brief length of time. Cash, debtors, inventories, loans and advances, and pre-paid costs constitute the current assets.

- Miscellaneous Expenditures and Losses: Preliminary and pre-operative expenses that were not written off are included in the miscellaneous expenditures. Although a loss signifies a reduction in the owners' equity, it does not imply a reduction in the share capital. Instead, on the liabilities and assets sides of the balance sheet, share capital and losses are shown separately.

Balance Sheet: Report Form

I.	**Sources of Funds**
	1. Shareholders' Funds
	(a) Share Capital
	(b) Reserves & surplus
	2. Loan Funds
	(a) Secured loans
	(b) Unsecured loans
II.	**Application of Funds**
	(i) Fixed Assets
	(ii) Investments
	(iii) Current Assets, loans and advances
	Less: Current liabilities and provisions
	Net current assets
	(iv) Miscellaneous expenditure and losses

Profit and Loss Account

The profit and loss account is the second most important financial statement. It shows the income and costs for a specific period. The period is an accounting period/year, which runs from April to March. The profit and loss account is divided into two types: traditional account form and step form. The accounting report describes the revenue and cost items and the difference (net income) for a specific accounting period.

Simply presenting statistics/data in various financial statements does not provide the complete picture of a company's financial condition. However, financial statements that have been appropriately reviewed and understood can give helpful information about a company's performance. A variety of tools are used to extract information from financial statements when analysing them. The Ratio Analysis is the most often used tool.

Ratio Analysis

A financial ratio is a numerical connection that exists between two goods or variables. The three types of financial ratios are (I) liquidity ratios,

(II) leverage/capital structure ratios, and (III) profitability ratios.

Liquidity Ratios

Liquidity refers to the ability of a firm to meet its financial obligations in the short term which is less than a year. Specific ratios which indicate the liquidity of a firm are (i) Current Ratio, (ii) Acid Test Ratio, (iii) Turnover Ratios. It is based on the relationship between current assets and current liabilities.

$$\text{Current ratio} = \frac{Current.Assets}{Current.Liabilities}$$

The current ratio assesses a company's capacity to satisfy current liabilities with current assets. The higher the current ratio, the more short-term solvency there is (i.e. more significant is the number of rupees available per rupee of liability).

$$\text{Acid-test Ratio} = \frac{Quick.Assets}{Current.Liabilities}$$

Current assets, excluding inventory and prepaid costs, are referred to as quick assets. The acid-test ratio measures a company's capacity to turn current assets into cash rapidly enough to satisfy its current obligations. In general, a 1:1 ratio is thought to be adequate.

Turnover Ratios

Turnover ratios measure how quickly certain current assets are converted into cash or how efficiently a firm employs the assets. The critical turnover ratios are:

- Inventory Turnover Ratio,
- Debtors Turnover Ratio,
- Average Collection Period,
- Fixed Assets Turnover and
- Total Assets Turnover

$$\text{Inventory Turnover Ratio} = \frac{Cost of Goods Sold}{Average Inventoty}$$

Where sales minus gross profit is the cost of products sold. The simple average of opening and closing inventory is referred to as "average inventory." The inventory turnover ratio measures inventory management efficiency. The higher the ratio, the more effective inventory management is.

Debtors' Turnover Ratio = $\dfrac{Net\,Credit\,Sales}{Average\,Accounts\,Receivable\,(Debtors)}$

The ratio indicates how frequently accounts receivable (debtors) are turned over during the year. If the net credit sales figure is unavailable, the net sales figure should be used instead. The more debtors change hands, the more efficient credit management becomes.

Average Collection Period = $\dfrac{Average\,Debtors}{Average\,Daily\,Credit\,Sales}$

The average collection period is the number of days' worth of credit sales that debtors are locked in for (accounts receivable).

Please keep in mind that the Average Collection Period and the Turnover of Accounts Receivable (Debtors) are connected in the following way:

Average Collection Period = $\dfrac{365\,Days}{Debtors\,Turnover}$

The Fixed Assets Turnover Ratio quantifies the amount of money sold for every rupee invested in fixed assets. To put it another way, how well-fixed assets are used. It is preferable to have a higher ratio. The formula is as follows:

$$\text{Fixed Assets turnover ratio} = \frac{Net.Sales}{Net Fixed Assets}$$

The total asset turnover ratio evaluates the efficiency with which all types of assets are used.

$$\text{Total Assets turnover ratio} = \frac{Net.Sales}{Average Tot al Assets}$$

Leverage/Capital Structure Ratios

A company's long-term financial strength or soundness is determined by its ability to pay interest on time and refund principle on due dates or at maturity. Leverage or capital structure ratios can be used to assess a company's long-term solvency. In general, there are two types of ratios: First, there are the ratios that are generated from the balance sheet and are based on the connection between borrowed money and owner's capital. Debt to equity and debt to asset ratios are two examples of such ratios. Second, the interest coverage ratio and debt service coverage ratio are coverage ratios for leverage risk, and they are derived from the Profit and Loss Account.

The debt-to-equity ratio measures the relative contributions of creditors and owners to the business's financing.

$$\text{Debt-Equity ratio} = \frac{Debt}{Equity}$$

From industry to industry, the desired/ideal percentage of the two components (high or low ratio) varies.

Total debt is made up of long-term debt as well as current obligations. Thus, permanent capital and current liabilities make up the overall assets.

$$\text{Debt-Asset Ratio} = \frac{Total\ Debt}{Total\ Assets}$$

The second set of ratios, known as coverage ratios, assesses the link between the firm's operating profits and third-party claims.

$$\text{Interest Coverage ratio} = \frac{Earnings\ Before\ Interest\ and\ Taxes}{Interest}$$

The higher the interest coverage ratio, the more capable the company is of meeting its interest obligations. Lenders use this ratio to determine a company's debt servicing capabilities.

The Debt Payment Coverage Ratio (DSCR) is a more complete and accurate method of calculating a company's debt service capability. Financial institutions calculate the average DSCR during the time during which the project's term loan is repayable. The following is how the Debt Service Coverage Ratio is defined:

$$\frac{Profit.after.tax + Depreciation + OtherNoncashExpenditure + Interest.on.term.loan}{Interest\ on\ term\ loan + Repayment\ of\ term\ loan}$$

Profitability Ratios

The following profitability ratios are used to assess a company's profitability and operational/management efficiency:

(i) Gross Profit Ratio = $\dfrac{Gross\ Profit}{Net\ Sales}$

(ii) Net Profit Ratio = $\dfrac{Net\ Profit}{Net\ Sales}$

Some of the profitability ratios related to investments are:

(iii) Return on Total Assets = $\dfrac{Net\ Income}{Average\ Total\ Assets}$

(iv) Return on Capital Employed = $\dfrac{Net\ Profit}{Capital\ Employed}$

(Here, Capital Employed = Fixed Assets + Current Assets - Current Liabilities)

Return on Shareholders' Equity = $\dfrac{Net\ Income\ After\ Tax}{Average\ Total\ Shareholders'\ Equity\ or\ NetWorth}$

(Net worth includes Shareholders' equity capital plus reserves and surplus)

A typical (equity) shareholder has only a residual claim on a company's profits and assets, i.e., the equity shareholders get a distribution of profits or assets only after the rights of creditors and preference shareholders have been completely satisfied. Thus, return on equity is a metric that reflects his well-being. Other methods for calculating return on shareholders' equity include:

Earnings Per Share (EPS): EPS is a metric that quantifies the profit available to equity owners per share, or the amount they may earn on each share owned. Divide the earnings available to shareholders by the number of outstanding shares to arrive at this figure. Net earnings after taxes and preference dividends are used to calculate the profits accessible to regular shareholders.

It indicates the value of equity in the Market:

$$EPS = \frac{Net\ Profit}{Number\ of\ Ordinary\ Shares\ Outstanding}$$

$$\text{Price-earnings ratios} = P/E\ Ratio = \frac{Market\ Price\ per\ Share}{EPS}$$

Chapter 14

Clearing and Settlement

All deals completed on the NSE's futures and options (F&O) sector are cleared and settled by the National Securities Clearing Corporation Limited (NSCCL). It also serves as the legal counterparty to all F&O deals and ensures their financial resolution. NSCCL conducts clearing and settlement activities in the F&O segment with the assistance of the following entities:

- Members of the clearing: The Clearing Member (CM) is primarily responsible for the following tasks:

  o Clearing: Calculating all of his TM's responsibilities, i.e. finding positions to settle.

  o Settlement: Dealing with the actual transaction. All Futures and Options contracts are currently cash settled.

- Risk Management: Setting position limits for each TM based on upfront deposits/margins and continuously monitoring positions.

Some members in the F&O segment, known as self-clearing members, clear and settle their trades exclusively on their clients' accounts or behalf. Some people are referred to as trading member–cum–clearing member (TM-CM) since they clear and settle their trades and other people's trades (TMs). Furthermore, professional clearing members (PCM) are a unique type of member who clear and settle deals performed by TMs but do not trade themselves. Members clearing their own and others' transactions and PCMs are obliged to bring in extra security deposits for each TM whose trades they are clearing and settling.

Clearing Member Eligibility Norms

- Net worth of at least Rs. 300 lakh. The net worth requirement for a CM who clears and settles only deals executed by him is Rs. 100 lakh.

- Deposit of Rs. 50 lakh to NSCCL, which forms the Base Minimum Capital (BMC) of the CM.

- Additional incremental deposits of Rs.10 lakh to NSCCL for each additional TM if the CM undertakes to clear and settle deals for other TMs.

- Clearing banks: Funds settlement takes place through clearing banks. For settlement, all clearing members must open a separate bank account with NSCCL designated clearing bank for the F&O segment. The Clearing and Settlement process comprises of the following three main activities:

    o Clearing

    o Settlement

    o Risk Management

Clearing Mechanism

Working out open positions and duties of clearing (self-clearing/trading-cum-clearing/professional clearing) members is the first stage in the clearing process (CMs). A CM's open positions are calculated by adding the open positions of all trading members (TMs) and custodial participants (CPs) clearing via him in the contracts they have traded. A TM's open position is calculated by adding his open position and his customers' open positions in the contracts they have traded. TMS designate orders as proprietary or client while entering them on the trading system using the 'Pro/Cli' indication on the order entry screen. For each contract, proprietary positions are computed on a net basis (buy-sell), and client positions are determined by adding the net positions of each customer, i.e., a buy transaction is offset by a sell trade, and a purchase trade offsets a sale trade. Thus, the total of a TM's proprietary open position, client open long position, and client open short position is the open position.

Settlement Mechanism

The settlement amount for a CM is netted across all their TMs/clients regarding their obligations on MTM, premium, and exercise settlement.

Daily Premium Settlement

A buyer of an option is responsible for paying the premium on the options he has acquired. Similarly, the option seller is entitled to the premium for the option he has sold. Therefore, the net premium payable or receivable amount for each customer for each option contract is calculated by netting the premium payment and receivable amounts.

Final Exercise Settlement

On the expiry day of an option contract, a final exercise settlement is made for all open extended in-the-money strike price options open after trading hours. On a random basis, all of these long positions are executed and automatically assigned to short positions in option contracts with the same series. Thus, the exercise settlement value per unit of the option will be received by the investor who has long in-the-money options on the expiry date from the investor who is short on the option.

Exercise Settlement Computation

All open long positions at in-the-money strike prices in option contracts with the same series are automatically executed on the expiry day and allocated to short positions in option contracts with the same series on a random basis. On the expiry day of the option contract, NSCCL automatically exercises all open long in-the-money positions in the expiring month options contract. The exercise settlement price is the underlying (index security closing)'s price on the option contract's expiry day. The difference between the strike price and the final settlement price of the applicable option contract is the exercise settlement value. The difference between the final settlement price and the strike price for each unit of the underlying conveyed by the option contract is the exercise settlement value receivable by a buyer for call options and the difference between the strike price and the final settlement price for each unit of the underlying conveyed by the option contract for put options. Option exercises are currently settled by cash payment rather than delivery of securities. The following formula is used to calculate the exercise settlement value for each unit of the exercised contract: Call options = Strike price — The closing price of the security on the day of exercise Put options = Strike price — The security's closing price on the day of exercise. On the expiration day, the underlying security's closing price is used. On T + 1 day (T = exercise date), the exercise settlement amount is debited/credited to the applicable CMs clearing bank account.

Chapter 15

Measures of Central Tendency

An average is a typical value, or representative, of a set of given data. Since such typical values tend to lie centrally within a set of data arranged according to magnitude, averages are also called measures of central tendency.

Mean

Mean is an average value of a set of values. It indicates the central value of the overall population. It equals the sum of all the values over (divided by) the number of observations. It is also known as the arithmetic mean. The arithmetic mean, or briefly, the mean, of a set of N numbers $X_1, X_2, X_3,..., X_n$ is denoted by X (read "X bar") and is defined as:

$$\overline{X} = \frac{X_1 + X_2 + X_3 + ... X_N}{N} = \frac{\sum_{j=1}^{N} X_j}{N} = \frac{\sum X}{N}$$

Example:

The arithmetic mean of the numbers 8, 3, 5, 12, and 10 is:

$$\overline{X} = \frac{8+3+5+2+12+10}{5} = \frac{38}{5} = 7.6$$

The weighted Arithmetic mean.

The mean can be calculated either without or with weights. The weighted mean is calculated by multiplying and summing each value (X_1, X_2, X_3,..., X_n) with the weights (w_1, w_2,..., w_n). Each weight is determined by the priority or relevance assigned to each value. In this situation, the weighted arithmetic mean is used.

$$\overline{X} = \frac{w_1 X_1 + w_2 X_2 + ... + w_n X_N}{w_1 + w_2 + ... w_n} = \frac{\sum wX}{\sum w}$$

Example:

If a final examination is weighted three times as much as each of the two internal assignments in a course, and a student receives an 85 on the final test and 70 and 90 on the internal assignments, the mean grade is:

$$\overline{X} = \frac{(1)(70)+(1)(90)+(3)(85)}{1+1+3} = \frac{415}{5} = 83$$

Thus, it is simply the sum of the weighted value of each observation.

The Geometric Mean (GM) is theoretically the optimum average for calculating returns on assets.

The Nth root of the product of the numbers is the geometric mean, G, of a set of N positive integers:

$$G = \sqrt[N]{X_1 X_2 X_3 .... X_n}$$

Example:

The geometric mean of two, four, and eight are:

$$G = \sqrt[3]{(2)(4)(8)} = \sqrt[3]{64} = 4.$$

The square root is used if there are two things; cube root is used if there are three items, and so on. The geometric mean may be calculated using either the logarithmic approach or a calculator.

Variance and Standard Deviation

Variance: An event's occurrence may differ from the mean or an expected value. A variance may be used to measure the spread of such events around the anticipated value. As a result, variance equals the average of the squares of each value's departure from the mean. It can be written as:

$$\text{Variance} = s^2 = \text{OR } \sigma^2 = \frac{\sum_{j=1}^{N}(X_j - \overline{X})^2}{N} = \frac{\sum(X - \overline{X})^2}{N} = \frac{\sum x^2}{N}$$

Coefficient of Variation

Complete dispersion is the natural dispersion/variation as assessed by standard deviation. On the other hand, relative dispersion offers a sense of absolute dispersion concerning the mean/average. In other terms, the relative dispersion is called 'coefficient of dispersion' or 'coefficient of variation' if the absolute dispersion is the standard deviation (σ) and the average is the mean (X). (V). It is provided by:

$$V = \frac{\sigma}{X}$$

www.ingramcontent.com/pod-product-compliance
Lightning Source LLC
Chambersburg PA
CBHW030913180526
45163CB00004B/1821